The Great APES

by Ariana Melzer

MW01109168

Scott Foresman
is an imprint of

PEARSON

Glenview, Illinois • Boston, Massachusetts • Chandler, Arizona
Upper Saddle River, New Jersey

Every effort has been made to secure permission and provide appropriate credit for photographic material. The publisher deeply regrets any omission and pledges to correct errors called to its attention in subsequent editions.

Unless otherwise acknowledged, all photographs are the property of Scott Foresman, a division of Pearson Education.

Photo locators denoted as follows: Top (T), Center (C), Bottom (B), Left (L), Right (R), Background (Bkgd)

Opener: Photo Studio; 1 Corbis; 3 ©Bryan Mullennix/Getty Images; 4 Corbis; 6 ©DK Images; 7 ©DK Images; 8 ©DK Images; 9 Corbis, ©DK Images; 10 ©DK Images; 11 Brand X Pictures; 12 Digital Vision; 14 Corbis; 16 Corbis; 18 Corbis; 19 Brand X Pictures; 20 Corbis; 21 ©DK Images; 22 Corbis

ISBN 13: 978-0-328-52616-1
ISBN 10:   0-328-52616-9

Copyright © by Pearson Education, Inc., or its affiliates. All rights reserved.
Printed in the United States of America. This publication is protected by copyright, and permission should be obtained from the publisher prior to any prohibited reproduction, storage in a retrieval system, or transmission in any form or by any means, electronic, mechanical, photocopying, recording, or likewise. For information regarding permissions, write to Pearson Curriculum Rights & Permissions, One Lake Street, Upper Saddle River, New Jersey 07458.

Pearson® is a trademark, in the U.S. and/or in other countries, of Pearson plc or its affiliates.

Scott Foresman® is a trademark, in the U.S. and/or in other countries, of Pearson Education, Inc., or its affiliates.

3 4 5 6 7 8 9 10 V0N4 13 12 11 10

The Great Apes

The great apes—orangutans, gorillas, chimpanzees, and bonobos—live in Africa and Asia. Studying the great apes tells us many things about the history of these animals and the world we live in. Scientists have spent many years studying the great apes. Among the most well-known of these scientists are Jane Goodall, Dian Fossey, and Biruté Galdikas, all of whom worked with great apes in Africa and Asia.

Orangutan

Bonobo

Gorilla

3

The great apes look very different from one another, but they have several things in common. All apes have a large brain in proportion to their body size. They have good eyesight and are able to see in three dimensions, which not all animals can do. Apes have arms that are quite long, usually longer than their legs. Their feet can grasp objects because their big toes, just like their thumbs, are opposable. An opposable toe or thumb is one that can move to touch the other toes or fingers.

Apes have a few remarkable behaviors in common too. All apes will eat certain minerals, clays, or plants to cure illnesses. Apes groom themselves and often each other, using their fingers and teeth to comb and clean their fur and skin. This keeps their fur and skin healthy.

These apes are feasting on plants.

Orangutans

Orangutans live in tropical rain forests on the islands of Borneo and Sumatra. The native language of these islands is Malay. In the Malay language, the word *orangutan* means "man of the forest."

Whether they live in Borneo or Sumatra, all orangutans have long fur that is either brown or red in color. The orangutans of Sumatra usually live at higher altitudes, where they rely on their fur for warmth.

It is easy to tell male and female orangutans apart, because males are often twice as large. Orangutans range between four and five feet in height and between seventy-five and two hundred pounds in weight. Male orangutans also have two special features on their faces: large cheek pads and a large throat sac.

Orangutan populations are still found in the wild on the Indonesian islands of Borneo and Sumatra.

Orangutans spend their days in the trees, eating the fruits that grow there. They live between thirty and ninety feet up in the air, in the part of the rain forest known as the middle canopy. One of their favorite fruits is the fig. When fruit is not available, orangutans eat bark and leaves.

Orangutans move from tree to tree by brachiating, or swinging on their long arms from branch to branch. Their opposable toes help them grab branches too. Sometimes orangutans will hang upside down from branches to reach fruit or leaves. But this can be dangerous for the orangutans, because they risk falling. Scientists have found orangutan skeletons that show bone breaks.

Since orangutans live in trees, they are usually safe from predators. They do not need to live in a group for protection. Adult orangutans usually spend time alone, but female orangutans keep their babies with them. A baby orangutan will stay with its mother until it is about five or six years old.

These apes sleep alone, with the exception of a mother and her young. Each orangutan weaves a nest from leaves and branches to sleep in at night. Can you imagine making a new bed every night?

Orangutans use their opposable thumbs and toes to grasp fruit and tree branches.

Orangutans are very smart creatures. One of the ways that they display their intelligence is through their many uses of leaves. Orangutans use leaves to shield themselves from rain or sunlight and to make roofs for their nests. Orangutans use leaves to wipe leftover food from their faces. They also use leaves to drink water from. They even wrap their hands in leaves for protection from thorns!

These apes also have excellent memories. One of their favorite foods, figs, is only in season at certain times of the year. But orangutans remember when figs are in season and return to the trees at that time to eat the figs.

Orangutans make more than a dozen different sounds. The male's large throat sac allows him to make a loud grumble or roar called a long call. It can be heard more than half a mile away! These calls tell other orangutans where he is.

Orangutans also make a sound called the kiss-squeak. They use this sound to show that they are angry or annoyed. In addition to making this sound, orangutans may break branches and throw them to the ground to scare enemies.

Orangutans are hard to study because they live in the trees, so scientists are still learning more about them.

Even though most orangutans live alone, they make sounds to communicate with other orangutans living nearby.

Gorillas

Another great ape is the gorilla. Before they were closely studied, gorillas were often misunderstood by humans. Some people thought that they were aggressive and vicious. Now we know that this is not true. Gorillas are actually peaceful primates who do not attack unless they are provoked or startled. They spend most of their time eating, resting, and sleeping in the mountains and lowlands of Africa.

This gorilla is using her knuckles to walk.

A gorilla's nose is unique. No two gorillas have the same nose print.

Gorillas are the largest primates on Earth. They range in height from five to six feet. Males can weigh up to six hundred pounds and females can weigh up to three hundred pounds. Their arm span can grow to almost ten feet. Gorillas have powerful upper bodies but, unlike orangutans, they rarely climb trees. They usually use their knuckles to walk on all fours, but they can stand up and run if they need to.

Most gorillas have black fur, though some have a brownish-gray coat. Their faces, the palms of their hands, and the soles of their feet do not have fur, and are also black. Gorillas that live in the mountains have long, thick coats of fur that keep them warm. Lowland gorillas have short, thin coats. Gorillas also have unique nose prints. No two gorilla noses are alike! Researchers often take pictures of gorillas' faces so they can tell the gorillas apart.

Gorillas live in groups called troops. The oldest male gorilla is in charge of a troop. When a male gorilla reaches about fifteen years old, some of the fur on his back turns silver. This is why mature males are called silverbacks. A silverback can lead a troop for more than ten years. He is responsible for the safety of the entire group. He decides where the group will travel for food, when they will rest or eat, and where they will spend the night.

Gorillas rest when not eating.

In addition to the silverback, a younger male called a blackback is part of the troop. The rest of the troop is usually made up of two to thirty adult females and a number of youngsters who are less than eight years old. But the makeup of the troop can change. The blackback may leave to find another troop that he can take charge of. Female gorillas often switch troops when they grow up.

Gorillas might spend half of their days eating. A male gorilla can eat about fifty pounds of food in a single day! Gorillas get plenty of water because they eat so many plants. But they must move around their habitat to find enough to eat. Their grazing causes **stimulating** plant growth.

Just like orangutans, gorillas weave a new nest to sleep in each night. The silverback usually sleeps on the ground to protect the troop, while the others build nests in trees or bushes.

Gorillas may bare their teeth if they feel they are in some kind of danger.

Gorillas have many ways to communicate. They use different sounds and facial expressions. Some gorilla sounds include calls, hoots, grunts, coughs, burps, snorts, and chuckles. A gorilla's facial expression can show tension, stress, concentration, or a wish to play.

Youngsters usually chuckle while playing. Females often belch when content. Males often use calls to calm disputes between females in the troop.

If the silverback feels the troop is being threatened, he can be very expressive. He may roar loudly, beat his chest, break branches, and charge at intruders to demonstrate his strength.

Gorilla researchers noticed the incredible number of ways that gorillas in the wild communicate. They wondered if **captive** gorillas could be taught a new way to communicate. They decided to try to teach captive gorillas to use sign language, and it worked!

In 1971, a female lowland gorilla was born at the San Francisco Zoo. She was named Hanabi-Ko, which means "fireworks child" in Japanese. Today she is known as Koko.

Koko can communicate with people by making more than one thousand different signs. Some of the first signs Koko learned were for *food*, *drink*, and *more*.

Koko can understand more than two thousand spoken English words! She answers questions by using sign language to make statements of three to six words.

The gorilla Koko has learned many different ways to express herself through sign language. This person is showing how to make the sign for drink.

Chimpanzees and Bonobos

Other great apes that live in the forests and woodlands of Africa are chimpanzees and bonobos. These two species are very similar.

Scientists did not properly identify bonobos as a separate species until 1933. They were thought to be a kind of chimpanzee. Bonobos continue to be the least understood of the apes. Even their name is the subject of some debate. The name *bonobo* may be a misspelling of a town in Africa named Bolobo.

While only a little is known about bonobos, researchers such as Jane Goodall have studied chimpanzees for a very long time. Chimpanzees have dark fur covering all of their bodies except their faces, ears, hands, and the soles of their feet. They range in height from about three feet to more than five feet. Their arm span can be more than nine feet. Female chimpanzees can weigh as much as one hundred pounds, and males can weigh more. Male chimpanzees are also more muscular than females, although all chimpanzees are very strong.

Bonobos are thinner than chimpanzees. The fur on their heads is often parted down the middle. They can also walk on two feet much more easily than chimpanzees, but both species spend time in the trees.

Young chimpanzees may have pink or brown faces, while the faces of older chimpanzees are black.

Chimpanzees are very social animals.

Chimpanzees and bonobos are very social animals, and unlike orangutans, they need **companionship**. They live in large communities that can have as many as one hundred members. Sometimes, however, these big communities divide into smaller groups.

In general, male chimpanzees are dominant over the females and offspring. One strong male is usually the community leader. Bonobo communities, on the other hand, are run by females.

Like other great apes, chimpanzees build a new nest each night in the trees. All group members make their own nests, except for the young, who sleep with their mothers. Bonobos build nests too, but unlike other great apes, they will sometimes share their nests.

Chimpanzees are omnivores. This means they eat both plants and meat. Fruit makes up most of their diet, but chimpanzees will also hunt small monkeys or antelope. They eat termites and ants as well. Bonobos have a similar diet, consisting mostly of fruit, leaves, and seeds. Sometimes bonobos will eat meat, but they never actually hunt for it as chimpanzees do.

Chimpanzees make tools to help them get food and water. Chimpanzees in certain parts of Africa use stones as **primitive** hammers to crack shells. They also use tools to get termites and ants. They select a twig or vine to slip into the insect holes in the ground. When the insects crawl on the twigs, the chimpanzees lift the twig up and run their mouths over them. Both chimpanzees and bonobos put leaves together and use them as sponges to soak up water to drink. Bonobos also use leaves like orangutans do, to stay dry in the rain.

Using tools is an amazing chimpanzee behavior.

Chimpanzees bark, grunt, hoot, and scream to communicate. The most common call chimpanzees make is a pant-hoot, which they make when they are very excited. The pant-hoots are often mixed with other sounds, such as drumming on a tree. Young chimpanzees may whimper when they are nervous or separated from their mothers.

Chimpanzees use different sounds to communicate with each other about important things such as food and danger. Their danger calls can be heard miles away!

Bonobos chatter a lot of the time, though these sounds can only be heard up close. Male bonobos do something with sound that no other apes do. They take turns so they do not drown each other out!

Chimpanzees, like other apes, use facial expressions and body language to show their feelings. Chimpanzees show that they want to play by grinning and covering their upper teeth. They pout when they are upset. They even hug and hold hands with friends. Bonobos use touch to reassure and comfort each other.

Both bonobos and chimpanzees have been used in language studies, like the one involving Koko. They can also be taught to communicate using sign language.

Chimpanzees' faces are very expressive. What do you think these chimpanzees are trying to say?

21

Unfortunately, the number of great apes in the world is declining, and their **existence** is threatened. Apes and their natural habitats are in danger of disappearing due to growing human populations, logging, and poachers.

Sanctuaries have been created to try and protect their habitats. A sanctuary is a large area of land that is protected from development and hunting. Animals are moved there so that they can continue to thrive in the wild. Researchers often work in sanctuaries to study apes.

Efforts are being made to protect apes from various **ordeals,** such as being captured for trade. Some people capture apes and sell them to zoos or to people as pets. This can be tragic for the apes. Adult apes have been killed while trying to protect their babies from poachers. To discourage the trade of apes, it is illegal to own one as a pet.

It is amazing to think over all we have learned about great apes and their behaviors. They are very intelligent and can communicate with each other in ways scientists fifty years ago never knew anything about. It has only been through the hard work of dedicated scientists that we have learned so much about apes. But there is definitely more to learn. That is why we must continue to protect these amazing creatures.

We must protect the great apes and their habitats so that they can continue to grow and thrive.

Glossary

captive *adj.* kept in confinement.

companionship *n.* friendly feeling among companions; fellowship.

existence *n.* condition of being.

ordeals *n.* severe tests or experiences.

primitive *adj.* very early stage of development.

sanctuaries *n.* places of refuge or protection.

stimulating *adj.* lively; engaging.

6

8